Poems from a Secret Garden

Fred E. Beaulieu

Preface

Light and darkness, triumph and defeat, joy and suffering, hopes and dreams, faith and discouragement. These all reflect aspects of the human experience which poets have endeavored for centuries to express through the written word. It has always been their deepest longing to communicate these universal and timeless thoughts and emotions, insights and experiences in such a way that they resonate within those who read them.

Poetry transcends generations and geography, age and gender, nationality and economic standing, societal status and education level. Poetry is the end result of the heart and mind working together in creative harmony. It can be written with tears or with laughter, in yearning or in contentment, amidst turmoil or tranquility. It has the ability to weave its way through the very fabric of our emotions and captivate our imagination.

The poems in this collection represent my own attempt to express the human experience in all of its myriad manifestations. It is my hope that you may be able to relate to, and enjoy, some of the offerings presented herein.

Acknowledgements

I wish to sincerely thank all those who have, over the years, supported me with their comments and suggestions as I've labored to improve and refine my writings. There are also a notable few whose encouragement and belief in me provided the impetus to pursue and realize my dream of publishing this book. I gratefully acknowledge and thank these special friends and family members…Jill, Joanne, Christine, Julie, Debbie, Elizabeth, Gene, David, Lisa and many others (they know who they are)!

Comments regarding the poetry in this book can be emailed to the author at: fredbeaulieu58@gmail.com.

Fred E. Beaulieu
September 2014
Revised March 2020

Awaken

Awake, my heart
The dawn doth break
Which cleanses pure
All past mistakes

Take wing, thou birds
Of morning flight
And usher in
Yon shafts of light

Behold, my eye
The promise fair
Which drifts upon
The dewy air

Rejoice, my soul
For hope draws nigh
It sails upon
The virgin sky

Two Roads

'Tis seldom, in this world I tread,
Two roads doth e'er converge
'Twould be a source of joyful bliss
If ever they shouldst merge

The first, a path my mind beholds
Which gently winds and turns
'Tis for this lush pastoral road
My heart forever yearns

The second path, best known to me,
I travel day by day
'Tis rutted with life's broken dreams
And leads me oft astray

The span by which these roads diverge
Doth move me to complain
'Tis like a map which matches not
A crude and coarse terrain

I oft attempt, with stern resolve,
These paths to reconcile
And yet their distance waxes more
Upon each passing mile

I must accept the simple fact
These roads may ne'er be wed
And naught I do can cease or slow
Their e'er increasing spread

All of my tomorrows

All of my tomorrows

will never be as sweet

as even one of my yesterdays

for one reason alone...

you were in my yesterdays

3

Halcyon Days

How bright, the autumn stars once shone
They burned as if for us alone
The silver harvest moon ablaze
With radiant grace and glistening haze

So soft, the snowy shawl that fell
Encasing earth with winter's spell
And long beguiling tranquil nights
Adorned by distant Northern Lights

How vibrant was the spring's rebirth
Arousing hope from slumb'ring earth
When nature's hand would fair bestow
The flower's bloom and river's flow

So dulcet were the summer songs
Resounding through the daylight long
Then twilight drew its sable cloak
And masked the whispered words we spoke

How distant are those halcyon days
'Tis where my thoughts so often stray
I long to sail those seas once more
And berth my ship along their shores

Alas, those tides are far removed
Beyond the coves which lulled and soothed
No vessel sails which can attain
Safe passage to those lost domains

At night, when drifting 'neath the stars
I chart my course for ports afar
And yet, whatever coasts draw nigh
They'll ne'er surpass the ones gone by

The sun hath set

Oh heart, my heart, why weepest so?
The sun hath set, the moon is low
The cooling autumn winds now blow
Which herald soon the coming snow

Oh heart, dear tender heart of mine
Those summer days fall fast behind
We'll drink no more September's wine
Nor bask in August's dreams divine

My heart, take pause and reminisce
On May and June's emergent bliss
I pray thee heart, be not remiss
To savor autumn's parting kiss

Come Hither

Come hither, sweet love, as I whisper my vows
Reclining 'neath blossoms of April's fresh boughs
The night passes quickly so let us make haste
To revel in pleasures of rapture's foretaste

The moonlight is full in this dew laden glade
Where young vestal maidens once gathered and played
No troubles intrude on this sanctified hour
Where soon we'll partake of the sweet and the sour

I'll read to thee Keats while a breeze turns the page
Transporting us back to that innocent age
And fragrant aromas that waft through the night
Anoint us with perfumes that stir our delight

The brush of thy fingertips soft cross my brow
Instills in me joys I've not known until now
The sight of your trembling lips close to mine
Awakens a passion of fervent design

Thy beauty enfolds me like seraphim wings
Portraying the comfort that paradise brings
Among all the treasures of heavenly charms
None greater exist than to lie in thine arms

The Hiding Place

While treading wooded paths at dawn
I chanced upon a trembling fawn
'Twas hidden in the summer brush
Attended by the hermit thrush

I asked the deer "Why hidest here?
The summer's days fast disappear
The forest glen doth call thy name
'Tis time to rise and seek thy claim"

The yearling said "I dare not stir
For dire harm may swift occur
Tho woodlands bear a pleasant face
Betrayal lies beneath its grace

I've suffered twice the hunter's snare
And lay three nights in dark despair
I scarce escaped, as helpless prey,
The savage beasts which roam the day

I hear the meadow's jubilee
And yet, those birds sing not for me.
I'll make my bed in brush obscured
Where safety's hedge will be assured"

I turned and left that hidden glade
To bask in nature's serenade
The rising sun brought forth the dawn
Yet could not reach the sheltered fawn

I then recalled a distant truth
A proverb from my days of youth
"Far better 'tis to risk the fall
Than ne'er attempt the leap at all"

Ghostly Realms

Pray tell me, ghosts of poets past
Pertaining to thy works so vast
How touchest thou the souls of men
With naught but paper, ink and pen

What kindled flame within thee burns
That chronicles our hearts' concerns
And bares those hidden joys and pain
Which course through every reader's vein

I pray thee, let thy secrets spill
And touch my forlorn yearning quill
Perchance to write some ageless verse
And through thy ghostly realms traverse

Secret Heart

'Neath winter's snow-clad mantle
Past autumn's last farewell
Encased by summer's harbour
A secret heart doth dwell

Within a tender bosom
Where whispered hopes are breathed
Surrounded by desires
A secret heart is sheathed

Beyond the distant valleys
Beside a rippling stream
Above the sacred mountains
A secret heart doth dream

'Tis beating with a rhythm
That none may comprehend
Too quickly does it suffer
Too slowly does it mend

Anointed by the perfume
That flows from sorrow's tears
Its eyes turned towards the morrow
In hopes of brighter years

It yearns for love's fulfillment
To yield its holy shore
It longs to be, above all else,
A secret heart no more

After The Ball

After the ball is over
After the dancers have gone
After the echoes of music have faded
While evening approaches the dawn

Memories hover like phantoms
Fragrances linger like rain
Unfulfilled dreams of romance lie abandoned
Like half empty flutes of champagne

Fantasies litter the dance floor
Where gowns and tuxedos convened
Festive adornments hang lifeless and limp
Where the secrets of love had been gleaned

Laughter had sprinkled the ballroom
Gaiety sang through the night
Starlight had mingled with promising words
Of desire and passion's delight

Glasses were lifted in tribute
Enchantment illumined each face
The terrace encounters in moonlit attire
Were cloaked by a whispered embrace

But now all the tables are empty
And silence enshrouds every booth
The laughter has died and the masks are discarded
Like innocent days of our youth

No longer does rapture enamour
Nor ecstasy flutter the heart
No longer does elegant splendor preside
Nor its regal pronouncements impart

The strolls in the garden have ended
No carriage remains on the grounds
The fountains have ceased from their night serenades
Of melodious cascading sounds

~

After the ball is over
After the candles have burned
All that remains is a bittersweet hope
That the music will one day return

Reflections of Tranquility

I walked along the ocean's shore and greatly mulled thereof
The magnitude and endless breadth of earth and sky above
The grains of sand along its coast and droplets in the sea
Were not unlike the hopes and prayers of all humanity

I then regarded seaside cliffs ascending heights unscaled
With rocks that formed the craggy base reflecting dreams that failed
The frothy surf was crashing 'gainst those jagged stones below
Like waves of tribulation borne of nature's ebb and flow

The distant mountains rose to glean the counsel of the sky
Where mortal aspirations strive to reach those realms on high
Each cloud that sailed in placid ease conveyed tranquility
Their proud procession marching forth in graceful majesty

As night began its pilgrimage from temples in the east
The moon arose to claim its throne among the starry priests
Their lanterns shone upon the earth to spark a hope in men
As silver-hued reminders that the day will break again

The dew on every blade of grass, as dawn revealed her face,
Were tears of unrepentant joy for daylight's fresh embrace
And warmth that spread across the fields from vibrant skies above
Portrayed the Savior's faithful vow to bathe us in His love

Where does love go?

Where does love go to when love goes away?
Why does it wander and not choose to stay?

Does it get restless, offended or bored?
Does it seek riches or other rewards?

Is it in search of some noble campaign?
Or off to discover a grander domain?

Does it remember the times that we shared?
The walks in the moonlight, the kiss on the stairs

Love has been gone now too long to recall
It surely must not have been love after all

If Only Words

If only words could ease the gloom
Restore a flower's faded bloom
Dispel a dark and somber mood
Awaken dreams you once pursued

If only words could bring to light
A spark of hope to ease your plight
A faith in future's promise bright
Rekindled joy in earth's delights

If only words could change the past
Erase regrets and words miscast
Illuminate a darkened road
And guide you to a safe abode

If only words could tears abate
Relieve a heart's oppressive weight
Revive the hope of summer's bliss
Recall the spell of love's first kiss

I pledge instead an outstretched hand
An ear to hear and understand
A shoulder, when the teardrops flow
Compassion, when the lamp burns low

February

February...

The slow,
labored march of

shackled days

wearily progressing
through weeks
of muted haze.

Imprisoned by ceilings
of oppressive
granite shrouds

And walls
of dull gray
emptiness.

Amid desperate,
fatigued pleas
for pardon,

my spirit succumbs
to the relentless
stifling
weight
of February

...and cries for April

Paean to Childhood

The path through the woods
Where I played as a child
Is barely apparent
With brush growing wild

It's hardly the sight
That my mind recollects
Yet still I press onward
As mem'ry directs

I follow this leading
Entangled and snared
Past thickets and glades where
Adventures were shared

I cannot say clearly
What force drew me hence
To mount up and straddle
This old crooked fence

From whence, as a lad,
I had fallen and sprained
My pride and my ankle
Both woefully pained

And yet, I remounted,
To chasten and break,
That bronco which cast me
Aside in his wake

And there, on a tree trunk,
A board remains nailed
A step to a platform
Which once I had scaled

Ascending towards heaven
Which formerly held
A rickety tree fort
Where soldiers had dwelled

Or Vikings or pirates
From Norway or Spain
Or Saxons in battle
'gainst King Charlemagne

Then further beyond
Past the black walnut hill
I tread towards that region
That tempted free will

Its fruit was forbidden
Yet still it attracts
The Siren Song lure
Of the railroad tracks

Descending the hillside
I try to go slow
But stumble and skid
To the gravel below

And standing there motionless
Lost in my thought
I wonder what manner of
Answers I sought

Surveying the tracks
From the west to the east
I reminisce long
On that great iron beast

Then placing my foot
On that worn steely rail
I venture to balance
And pass through time's veil

My mind bridged the chasm
Between now and then
I walk down that tightrope
A child once again

I stroll for a mile
Like a vagabond tramp
In search of a suitable
Site to encamp

The sun started setting
The day was adjourned
The curtain had closed
It was time to return

While setting out homeward
A thought crossed my mind
I turned back towards ages
I'd just left behind

In tribute to childhood
Which none can bring back
A penny I placed
On that railroad track

Ode to spring

While sitting on a riverbank observing nature's flow
I watched as spring revived the melting water's rush below
A measure of eternity was swirling in that stream
As currents beat in rhythm to creation's vibrant theme

I lingered on that river's edge as rapids hurried by
Reflecting sunlight's sparkling bliss beneath a sapphire sky
Yet as the course meandered towards its home beyond the bend
I knew that in December's grip, the stream would freeze again

The virgin air was pulsing with the beat of feathered wings
As flocks began returning like a throng of exiled kings
In pageantry triumphant, they reclaimed their kingdom's prize
While voicing proclamations through the lofty April skies

My hapless soul rejoiced to hear their canticles of praise
Those sweetly echoed hymns upon the gusts of vernal days
Yet in the midst of joyfulness, my mind could not ignore
That when leaves of autumn fell, their songs would ring no more

I watched the sun descend beyond horizon's furthest peak
The sky awash in pigments tinged with Heaven's deep mystique
My spirit ached in witness to a portrait so divine
As nature hushed and bowed her head before this sacred shrine

As darkness flooded forest glens and heav'nly lights arose
The shadows shared those secrets which the day cannot disclose
Yet though the evening casts a spell so beautiful and strong
I knew when winter reappeared these nights would grow so long

I wish for spring to linger and for time to slow its pace
To lie beneath the willows in a lover's warm embrace
When northern winds arrive conveying clouds of ashen gray
My heart will hide in April till December fades away

Love Lost

There are times when I sit by my window at night
Where I gaze at the moon and the mist of its light
There are times when I ponder on what might have been
As I wonder if ever I'll see you again

Through many a rainfall and fierce summer storms
I cling to those mem'ries which comfort and warm
Through many a snowfall and winter's cold blast
My heart remains captive in seasons long passed

There were times when I walked through the woods as a boy
When the dreams of my youth overwhelmed me with joy
There were times I believed all my dreams had come true
In the days of enchantment, when first I met you

When autumns and springtime all pass in their turn
When stars lose their luster my love will still burn
Should meadows and mountains no longer endure
I promise you always a love strong and pure

There are times when I'm bold, even reckless and wild
There are times all alone when I weep as a child
There are times when it's hard to be strong as I should
Like the times I'm reminded you're absent for good

When heaven and earth become shadow and sand
When the time for an end to all things is at hand
One light shall remain which can ne'er fade away
From the fire which rages inside me this day

~

There are times when I sit by my window at night
Where I gaze at the moon and the mist of its light
There are times of reflection on all I've come through
But the times I miss most are my moments with you

When Dreams Fail

O dawn,
Fragile dawn
With thy promise anew
'Tis your hollow illusion
We mortals pursue

O day,
Fickle day
Thou hast teased me once more
Like a desolate sky
Through which no bird doth soar

O eve,
Haunting eve
When thy wraiths coalesce
To thy legions of shadows
My hopes acquiesce

O night,
Wretched night
From whence torments emerge
Midst the stillness of thoughts
And the absence of words

O life,
Bitter life
I lie broken and spent
Off thy coasts lay those rocks
I could not circumvent

The Mountain Lodge

I love to spend my winters in this lodge atop the ridge
It lies beyond the frozen creek and past the covered bridge
It's nestled in the mountains far beyond the nearest town
And sits among the pine trees like a jewel atop a crown

This lodge had been abandoned by its owners from the east
Who siphoned all the profits like a glutton at a feast
They couldn't see the value in the beauty all around
But focused on their revenues and ran the ship aground

I found this hidden treasure in a state of bleak despair
Neglected by its steward and in broken disrepair
I bartered for its purchase and secured the lodge's deed
While vowing I'd restore it out of love and not from greed

Through several lengthy seasons I repaired my lofty prize
Though many thought me foolish, it was heaven in my eyes
I saw beyond the battered beams and panes of broken glass
Inspired by my vision of its elegance and class

I first rebuilt the shoring and the lumber that was cracked
Then buttressed the foundation with the girding that it lacked
I cleared the rooms of litter and debris from vacant years
The end result of apathy by heartless profiteers

I sanded, scrubbed and varnished to revive the faded wood
Amazed at all the damage that this structure had withstood
The outer deck was rotted so it had to be removed
But soon I built another that I felt was much improved

I then turned my attention to the fireplace inside
A masterpiece of stonework that was built with love and pride
I grieved at how the hearth had been neglected and debased
Lamenting at the senselessness behind this wanton waste

I took great care and effort reconstructing every piece
Through many restless days and nights my work would seldom cease
Then finally I finished and my labors were complete
A source of warmth and beauty for my mountainside retreat

I stood before the window as I gazed across the land
A breathless panorama made by God's own mighty hand
I watched a distant bull elk as it crossed a small ravine
Then through the gentle snowfall viewed an ambling wolverine

I saw a stealthy timber wolf, concealed and on the prowl
While high above the treetops soared a regal spotted owl
Below the mountain ridge I spied a timid snowshoe hare
Too far removed from cover or the safety of its lair

I love the charmed seclusion of this lodge among the pines
Its solitude and peace is where my weary soul reclines
Such majesty and splendor weaves a spell I've never known
Embracing me each winter as I sojourn here alone

The Curio Shoppe

While browsing through a local shop of rare and sundry notions
I chanced upon a curio which kindled strange emotions
An ageing book of photographs, an archived reminiscence
An album filled with bygone ghosts of antiquated essence

This frail collection caught my eye, a relic-filled possession
Obscured beneath the weight of years yet flush with rich impressions
It stood apart from all the other varied odd selections
The carvings, charms and tapestries; the antique doll collections

This brittle gift acquired that morn secured my rapt attention
Its shop-soiled pages wove a spell beyond my comprehension
These random scenes in monochrome unveiled the bygone ages
A mystic script of timeless prose inscribed upon life's pages

I found myself immersed each night within that world so distant
Responding to its haunting scenes, its summons so insistent
My captive mind would be enthralled with each enchanted viewing
Enticed by inner secrets which I could not cease pursuing

What joys and pleasures filled their days, what toils and consequences?
How did they face each painful trial that fate so oft dispenses?
Would anyone still recognize these faces, vast and varied?
Or are they merely phantoms which the sands of time have buried?

Might some descendent still recall their names or occupations?
Their daily struggles, hopes and dreams; their triumphs and
frustrations
What quests did they embark on, were they poor or educated?
What grand ambitions did they hold, and were they consummated?

Were pride and blessings flaunted like displays in a museum?
Were indiscretions buried like a padlocked mausoleum?
I'm certain there were romances propriety kept hidden
And surreptitious love affairs which custom had forbidden

In many ways, I'm sure their lives were not so much contrary
To present day humanity from birth to cemetery
Where poverty and privilege are duly represented
Where justice and inequities are lauded and lamented

And one day in the future, should another generation
Perchance obtain this archived photographic preservation
I wonder, would it speak to them with images eternal
In much the way it speaks to me, this tattered wordless journal

I store it on my bookshelf with an album I'm creating
A pictographic volume for a future age awaiting
A message in a bottle for time's undulating oceans
That may, one day, turn up within a shop of sundry notions

Secret Breeze

O, were I but a summer's breeze
To blow across your brow
And plant my fragrant kisses
As a blossom on your bough

Then would I find contentment
In my secret revelry
For you would laugh and toss your hair
Not knowing it was me

Just a Man

I've wanted to be chivalrous, a knight upon a steed
A gallant dashing stalwart who performs a noble deed
I've tried to be an intellect with words of depth sublime
Dispensing troves of wisdom which withstand the test of time

I strove for wealth and prominence, to woo you with success
Convinced a higher station would be certain to impress
Yet all of this was foolishness, which now at last I see
My quests were only fantasies of who I wished to be

I'm not a worldly voyager who's traveled to Nepal
A brave and mighty conqueror who'll answer when you call
A Byzantine crusader with a mission to pursue
I'm just a man who loves you with a simple heart that's true

Traveler's Tale

I've traveled for ages and seen many sights
Like merry old souls under starry bright nights
My journeys are quests for the love I once knew
Past sheep in the meadow and little boys blue

I've climbed every beanstalk in search of your heart
And wondered how was it, we drifted apart
Outside of the looking glass, all the king's men
Still ponder reflections of what might have been

I've stumbled through forests as blind as a mouse
In hopes of reclaiming our gingerbread house
Now all the king's horses have joined me to find
Those magical breadcrumbs we once left behind

Remember the times when our dreams would unfold?
Those days when our love would spin straw into gold
Now nothing remains but a cupboard that's bare
The porridge is cold and there's none left to share

As bridges in London continue to fall
The maids in a row try to help me recall
The secret to changing these tears into wine
Transporting me back to the days you were mine

While cats and their fiddles play melodies sweet
This storybook ending remains incomplete
In Neverland dreams where all fables come true
The man in the moon guides my footsteps to you

Look Not For Me

Look not for me hither
Look not for me yon
My journey now takes me
To regions beyond

I once lodged in safety
But dwell there no more
My ship has departed
Your long barren shore

Look not for me hither
Nor yonder as well
I've passed through the barrens
And bid them farewell

I've passed o'er the mountains
And brazened the sea
Descended the shoal cliffs
Of daunting degree

I roam as a stranger
In countries unknown
Through castles and courtyards
I travel alone

Look not for me hither
I shall not return
That chapter has ended
That page has been turned

Haunted

The old creaky manor stands grim and forlorn
The windows are boarded, the curtains are torn
No footsteps are heard on the floorboards inside
Where only the phantoms of passion reside

The ghost of your love roams the halls of my heart
It rises at dusk and is loath to depart
Past portraits of paradise, faded and drawn
Reminders of idyllic ages foregone

It glides past the chambers where romance once slept
But now hold the fragments of dreams left unswept
No music comes forth from the parlor downstairs
And silence abounds in the chapel of prayers

The dining room silver is tarnished and stained
Reminders of evenings when elegance reigned
The paths in the garden, where children once played,
Are absent the sounds of their sweet serenade

The ghost of your love haunts the depths of my soul
And cries with an anguish I cannot console
It echoes through corridors long since denied
The light of your presence to serve as my guide

I long to break free from this specter of old
Which fills every room with a presence so cold
Yet still does it linger, refusing to leave
Or grant me the peace of a lover's reprieve

Heritage

chase

giggle

tumble

roll roll roll

grab

squirm

tickle

squeal

love

...grandkids

Poem without Words

you are my poem without words

cadence and rhythm too beautiful to be constrained by mere stanza and verse

fluid measures unbound by the rigid confines of the printed page

sweeping elegance too elusive to be captured by scribe's quill

flowing streams of cascading rhymes faintly adorned with delicate inferences

you are my poem without words

I long to explore the depths of your hidden meanings

immerse myself in your subtle imagery

and bask in the elation of your ageless message

you are my poem without words

when compared to the revered sonnets of sage poets,

none can approach your delicate and graceful eloquence

in your presence I stand breathless and awestruck

forever inspired by the timeless nature of your perfect prose

you are my poem without words

...let me read you again

God Smiles

Sometimes

in the midst
of life's storms

God smiles

The day I met you

was one of those times

Autumn

Autumn

...That beautiful death

Hues and colors ablaze with splendor

Nature awash from one last breath of brilliance

...A tender farewell kiss

From a departing lover

Whose impassioned sonnets blanket the earth

...The wistful maiden who gazes at you longingly

Before fleeing through the forest

At the sound of approaching wolves

...The last dance of the ball

Where partners sway to and fro

Enchanted by the poignant rhythm of the final waltz

Foul Grave

Foul grave, thou art a brazen thief
That bringest waves of tortured grief
Thy coming fills the heart with woe
From Acheron's dark undertow

Foul grave, thy reach extends beyond
the hidden veil of earthly bonds
No pity shown for proffered pleas
From widowed brides on bended knees

Foul grave, thy fated bell that tolls
Resounds to summon hapless souls
And drags them to yon gaping maw
To satisfy thy heinous law

I hate thee with a holy wrath
From when thy visage crossed my path
And robbed this world of treasure dear
Conveyed beyond our mortal sphere

The prophets' dreams have long foretold
An age when hearts shall be consoled
The day of judgment draweth nigh
When even thou, foul grave, shall die

I'll Write No More

I'll write no more these empty words
That once did waft like soaring birds
And danced upon the printed page
Like actors on a parchment stage

I'll write no more such noble verse
Which quill and ink would once disburse
Extolling virtue's valiant quest
Of passion's warmth 'neath maiden's breast

I'll write no more of hearts remiss
Nor star-crossed lovers' final kiss
Of ships and trains and windswept fears
Or late night heartache's lonely tears

No more, this lame and feeble prose
Of halting rhymes will I compose
No more, these wretched words I'll write
'Neath harvest moon or lantern's light

I'll write no more, for words are vain
Their worth, I view with great disdain
Where once, their flow seemed pure and chaste,
They now appear the greatest waste

Secret Garden

(for Cheryl, wherever she may be)

That magical summer we shared 'neath the sky
I thought that my life had been blessed from on high
Our hearts shared a tune that we sang to the stars
Our passions ran deep and the whole world was ours

But just like a song of a failed romance
The melody ended, and so did our dance
Our story played out like a drama from school
Where you were the angel and I was the fool

Our love affair over, my dreams fell apart
For hopes can't be nurtured from desolate hearts
I treasured your photo, a joy from my past
Of beauty, refinement and grace unsurpassed

I tried to move on, dating girls that I met
Yet none of them ever could help me forget
I struggled through college, both aimless and lost
Adrift on a sea that was troubled and tossed

That summer I backpacked through Europe alone
And showed several people "my girlfriend back home"
At night in my tent I felt shame for my lies
Then fell asleep dreaming of stars in your eyes

A year after that I enlisted to fight
And wondered if you would be proud of "your knight"
I carried your photo to faraway fields
Yet even through battles, my heart never healed

When conflicts had ended, I came back to town
While wondering if you might still be around
I even drove back to the place where we met
And sat there for hours with ghosts of regret

A year or two later, I married my wife
Determined to forge on ahead with my life
We started a family and made all our plans
Yet found that you still held my heart in your hands

Your picture I hid in the attic above
A futile attempt at suppressing "first love"
Yet harder than storing your photo away
Was fighting those thoughts when my mind tried to stray

On hot sleepless nights I go up there alone
And open the trunk where my daydreams are sown
My wife knows I'm hiding a secret inside
Aware that it's something I'll never confide

When sometimes she asks if our love is still strong
I offer those words that I've used for so long
I think she's unsure of just how to surmise
That wistful and faraway look in my eyes

The years of my life have all quickly rolled by
My kids are now grown and have said their good-byes
I sit on my porch looking back on the past
Reflecting on trophies of life I've amassed

Yet still, after so many seasons apart,
I pull out your picture and pine in my heart
And wonder if ever you think of those days
When heaven was opened and skies were ablaze

I'll cherish you always, until my last breath
When angels attend to the hour of my death
Your vision exhorts me like grace from above
If not for that summer, I'd ne'er have known love

Let Me Lie

Let me lie in your arms till this madness subsides
When the torrents of tempests assail from all sides
Let your tender embrace be my refuge at night
When my barricades falter and courage takes flight

Like a fortress that promises safety's rewards
So I long for the peace that your bosom affords
Keep me sheltered from torments that ravage my mind
In my wretched exposure, defenseless and blind

Through my desperate sobs, I will whisper your name
As the one who absolves all my weakness and shame
Through my tear flooded eyes I will search for your face
In my quest for salvation, bestowed by your grace

I will cling to your love in my times of distress
As a child to his blanket when nightmares transgress
In the light of your comfort all shadows retreat
And dark dreams that oppress me succumb to defeat

In the day when my eyes shall awaken no more
When the angels escort me to Heaven's sweet shore
I will carry a solace throughout those blest lands
From the succor and love I received at your hands

A Dream's Demise

So thusly, does the story end
The dream has been destroyed
The chamber where my heart once beat
Lies barren, cold and void

How cruel the nameless fates can be
Capricious, harsh, unkind
How coldly shine the guiding stars
So sorely misaligned

"Injustice, offence, tragedy"
I scream and scream again
And rail in blind futility
'gainst angels, gods and men

What madness plagues the senses
When the heart is scorned and spurned
An unrequited love is like
A priceless gift returned

The need for love doth e'en surpass
The very will to live
Its absence is a trespass that
The heart cannot forgive

The dream has been abandoned
Like a tractor in the rain
A rusted souvenir of what
May never come again

Days of Uncertainty

What if the songbirds of morning were still
No welcoming promise of dreams to fulfill
What if the daybreak no longer renewed
Our wounded emotions and longings subdued

What if those mem'ries of halcyon days
Began to dissolve in a gray misty haze
Laughter of children in ghostly retreat
And triumphs of life overcome by defeat

How do we strive in the midst of such trials
With wellsprings of tears under counterfeit smiles
God, in His infinite wisdom, allows
Those harsh tribulations the heart disavows

What if, in autumn, the leaves did not turn
No harvest of colors which makes our hearts yearn
Days of uncertainty test and assail
Like breezes long absent from fishermen's sails

Sometimes the reasons are clouded from view
Enshrouding the answers we long to pursue
Desperate searches for meaning and truth
And solace long absent since days of our youth

Sometimes a heart has no strength to resist
Continual onslaughts that often persist
Unresolved questions at day's final end
Bring cold midnight vigils where poems are penned

Sometimes the moon has to struggle to rise
Arching through vacant and comfortless skies
Sometimes a candle's engulfed by the gloom
And sometimes the roses in spring fail to bloom

Letters Unsent

Contained within this shoebox lie those letters I once wrote
Which chronicle a time that now seems distant and remote
I've saved them as reminders of a passion that once bloomed
Throughout those fateful seasons where my heart was so consumed

The ones I wrote in April, in those days when first we met,
Were filled with idle chatter and an ease I'll not forget
I talked of random happenstance and life's mundane affairs
Of daily mediocrity and ordinary cares

The ones I wrote when May arrived were filled with something new
Some glimmers of awakening were slowly coming through
My words conveyed a brighter tone relating hopes and dreams
My pen was light and fanciful, replete with sanguine themes

Those dear and precious letters that I wrote the month of June
All spoke of passion's advent and two hearts that beat in tune
I wrote of kindred spirits and of love beneath the stars
Emboldened by the rapture of a romance such as ours

I wrote throughout the next three months with ecstasy divine
Inscribing on those pages all my deepest thoughts sublime
The energy that flowed so free enwrapped my very soul
For, after years of loneliness, my life at last felt whole

Then came that bleak September day, you bid my love farewell
Your final words resounding like a dull and aching knell
The letters from October all were stained with tears of grief
That fell in silent witness while I wrote in disbelief

The weary words I tried to pen, when came November's frost
Reflected resignation of a chance forever lost
Those letters sit unposted in this box I almost burned
Before that blest December, in the month that you returned

Canvas of Time

Time is the canvas upon which we paint
A mural of history passed
Imprints of infinite lives through the years
Humanity's archival cast

Time captures all from the moment of birth
Each action, response and intent
Angels of permanence pressed in the snow
Or handprints enshrined in cement

Acts and objectives determine the hues
And textures comprising our mark
Lackluster gray-scale or vibrant pastels
Though some are exceedingly dark

Time is a canvas which one day will end
Concluding when none shall expect
Earthly remembrances fade like the grass
Eternity never forgets

Looking back over the finished result
And tracing the steps that we trod
Have we enriched this concerted collage?
Or carelessly sketched a façade?

We are the artist, the pallet and brush
Determining what we prepare
Will we contribute a masterful work?
Or leave all our canvases bare?

Sad Days

They're sometimes known as 'sad days' for emotions they exude
Those short or lengthy intervals of melancholy moods
They bring a somber feeling as their harbinger arrives
Which often overshadows countless aspects of our lives

They may not be preceded by a triggering event
Some happenstance occurrence that evokes a dark descent
Yet still they fall upon us like an overwhelming tide
Which sweeps away our joy until their sullen waves subside

Their measure of intensity may sometimes wax and wane
Their source may be unknowable or hard to ascertain
It's possible they're products of some undetermined fears
Or maybe dreams unrealized we've wept about for years

We only know for certain that they come and go at will
These onerous intruders and the sadness they instill
We go about our daily lives with smiles upon our face
Concealing inner turbulence or hurts we can't erase

Some days are like a pestilence which withers and erodes
They take us down the detours of their dark and lonely roads
We disavow their presence and pretend that all is well
While trudging through a bleakness we're unable to dispel

They're sometimes known as 'sad days' when we feel like all is lost
When nothing seems to matter and our fragile ship is tossed
We fight to hold the tears inside while walking barren lands
In search of sanctuary or a soul who understands

45

All that she brings

When questioned why I love her so
I oft reply "I do not know"
'Tis like the song the robin sings
I love her for those joys she brings

She brings the rain on parched brown days
And rainbows midst the arid haze
Her moistened lips supplant the dust
And slake the thirst of earth's dry crust

She brings the breeze on summer eves
Which stirs the maple's laden leaves
Her breath abates the humid air
With gentle winds from autumn's lair

Her smile illumines gloomy nights
When stars are hid from earthly sight
Her eyes bring light that shames the dark
Like lantern's glow and lightning's spark

She brings a peace that calms my soul
When tempests rage and billows roll
I bring her naught but love's young seed
She smiles and says "'tis all I need"

Loneliness

How hollow rings the muted bell
Whose clapper does not toll
Nor peal its clarion timbre
'cross the distance of the knoll

I see the raven's silhouette
Against the waning moon
Its wings beat out the rhythm
Of a long-forsaken tune

The ghosts of masquerades gone by
Parade before my mind
Like wispy strands of gossamer
Yet sharply well-defined

How pallid are the colors
In the shadows of my room
A dank and musty sepulcher
That longs to be exhumed

Should You Come

And should you come in springtime
When the honeysuckles bloom
I'll make for you a garland
With a scent of sweet perfume

We'll wander through the woodlands
Where the cherry blossom grows
Then lay amongst the heather
For our blissful sweet repose

And should you come in summer
Like the tepid Spanish tides
I'll drape your bed with linens
Till the humid breeze subsides

I'll lace your room with jasmine
From the market down below
Then trim the courtyard lanterns
When the evening shadows grow

Or should you come in autumn
As the winds of change take hold
I'll tend the warming fires
While October days unfold

I'll weave you tales of romance
'Neath the crystal harvest moon
Then guard your ev'ning slumbers
Till the darkness turns to noon

But if you come in winter
May your Nordic guides be strong
And lead you though the mountains
To my arms where you belong

I'll keep a midnight vigil
For your torches from the north
And watch in prayerful silence
Till your caravans come forth

Anniversary Waltz

As evening descends on a small Midwest farm
The sky slowly reddens and dusk spreads its charm
While cares and concerns of the daytime take flight
Soon phantoms of present and past will unite

A light from the doorway spills out through the air
Revealing a figure descending the stairs
A rose in his hand, dressed in formal attire
And driven by dreams of impassioned desires

He heads round the back, past the old garden shed
Through rustling cornfields, towards what lies ahead
Then into a clearing of special design
To witness a vision of beauty divine

She's graced by a gown that he longs to embrace
And bears not a trace of ill health on her face
Approaching his spouse in this sanctified hour
He offers his gift of a single red flower

While crickets commence with their soft serenade
These lovers encircle the grass promenade
Then Japanese lanterns of fireflies take flight
To glitter the field and enrapture the night

As stars cast a glow from their stations on high
And fleeting black figures of birds whisper by
The dancers converge in a waltz, slow and long
And sway to the rhythm of nature's sweet song

Within this enchantment, the partners entwined,
The cares of this world are left so far behind
No words need be spoken, their eyes say it all
While dancing like guests at a grand royal ball

Too soon it is over, the lovers retreat
The man turns in silence, their hour complete
He heads for the farmhouse while tears stream his face
His heart bearing emptiness none can replace

For seven long years since his wife left his side
He's fought to continue while aching inside
Now all that sustains him are dreams of romance
And moments they share in a summer night's dance

(Letters to a) Dear Unknown

Today while I shopped near the old village square
I glanced through the crowds in the hopes you were there
I felt that I'd know, by the look on your face,
You also were seeking a lover's embrace

I browsed through the bookstore and stopped for a bite
Then, folding my napkin, I ventured to write
I left you a note just in case you were near
Recounting my dream of the day you'll appear

~

Today was a good day, my mood was upbeat
My work was productive, my tasks all complete
But when I arrived at my home late that night
I had no one waiting to share my delight

I made myself supper then tried to unwind
Yet rather than freedom, my heart felt confined
I longed to relate my success and good news
To hear your perspectives, your insights and views

~

Today was quite normal and not much transpired
My work was mundane and I felt uninspired
I wished we could meet at a local café
To share idle chatter and silly clichés

You'd listen intently and smile as I'd speak
Then brighten my mood with a kiss on the cheek
We'd laugh over nothing while others looked on
And linger about till our lunchtime was gone

~

Today I felt ill so I stayed home in bed
With thoughts of you floating around in my head
I wondered, if only you knew of my plight,
Then would you illumine my dark with your light

With poems and prose, would you sit by my side
And read me a tale of two lovers denied
Then lie for a while with your head on my chest
And gently depart when my eyes closed in rest

~

Today was a sad day, I felt quite depressed
It took half an hour just to get myself dressed
I drove around town in a downpour of rain
Discarding the smile I no longer could feign

I thought for a moment of how you might cope
If ever I faltered and forfeited hope
Would somehow you sense that a chance had been lost
If fate never smiled and our paths never crossed

~

The days are a blur as they pass swiftly by
They fold into years in the blink of an eye
Reflecting back over a lifetime alone
I yearn for the day you're no longer 'unknown'

The Brooding Night

How long, the brooding night's embrace
That hinders dawn's elusive face
How far removed, those realms of sleep
From eyes that long for slumber's keep

How empty lies the midnight air
Conveying not my fragile prayer
Where once the moon shone full and bright
Dull shadows now obscure its light

How absent is the night bird's voice
Which once did make my soul rejoice
Now heavy hangs the wounded heart
Which tempest winds have torn apart

Where hides the daybreak's promised bliss
Bestowed as if a lover's kiss?
Why flees the hope of joy restored
Through patient trust in faith's reward?

How long, the brooding night's embrace
Whose sorrow, time cannot erase
And mem'ries of those precious years
Fill sleepless hours with mournful tears

Yet Should I Die Tomorrow

Yet should I die tomorrow
Ere the breaking of the day
What legacy would linger
When my spirit slips away?

Would those who knew me sorrow
As they place me 'neath the earth?
Or chat in idle discourse
On the merits of my worth?

Would others be inspired
By the life I left behind?
Or were my moral principles
Too vague and undefined?

How often did I compromise
Those values I extolled?
Did truth and honor prove to be
A burden to uphold

Would friends and family wonder
If I passed through Heaven's gates?
Partaking of those joys within
Where blessed peace awaits

Or have I given cause for doubt
By living with disdain?
Forsaking my integrity
In selfish quests for gain

I think about these questions
As the twilight hours descend
And wonder how I'll answer
When my days are at an end

The Poem Unread

I chanced upon a poem rare
Amongst a bookstore's faded ware
'Twas in a volume, old and worn
Neglected, battered, shunned and torn

Some unknown writer penned such verse
With form and cadence so diverse
It caused my very heart to leap
And stirred my soul from restless sleep

'Twas not by Keats' nor Shelley's hand
Nor Wordsworth's pen, in fashion grand,
But by some lowly bard obscure
Yet touched with grace and candor pure

This single work enclosed therein
Did'st fan a flick'ring flame within
And tho his poem bore no name
Its beauty moved me just the same

It grieved me sore to contemplate
This author's lost and lonely fate
For such as these should take their place
With others whom our hearts embrace

It gave me pause to long reflect
On poets who deserve respect
But find themselves consigned instead
To languish on the shelves unread

Until the final moment

You ask with apprehension if my love will always last
As if it could be here today but then tomorrow past
None other have I loved before nor ever shall again
I've loved thee with a might surpassing that of other men

I'll love thee 'til the autumn kneels before December's throne
'til sweet October's afterglow dissolves to realms unknown
My love will yet endure until the end of life's embrace
Until that final moment which each mortal man must face

I'll love thee as death's footfall echoes soft outside my door
'til darkness falls across my face and breath remains no more
I'll love thee on that final trek across the Great Divide
Where time has no dominion and travails cannot abide

I'll love thee as the angels seek in vain to comprehend
The enigmatic beauty of a love that has no end
I'll love thee though eternity itself begins to wane
Yet even then, a beacon of my love shall still remain

Masquerade

We spoke at length as loneliness
And silhouettes converged
'midst dusk's encroaching shadows
As our masquerades emerged

Like skilled accomplished thespians
Our roles we deftly played
While conversation mingled
With the fruits of our charade

We laughed about fortuity
And life's capricious flow
Of random serendipity
And poets like Thoreau

We then discussed the theatre
Philosophy and art
The Bridge of Sighs in Venice
Aristotle and Descartes

Our idle chatter seemed to fill
The ever-present void
Yet vacuous pretensions
Still were tools that we employed

We tried to delve beyond those masks
That served to cloak and shield
But as each one was stripped away
Another was revealed

Our rendezvous concluded
As we echoed our goodbyes
Unsure if this encounter
Would be one we'd soon reprise

And if we met again some night
What scene might be portrayed?
Or would we just perpetuate
This endless masquerade

Marionette

you twirled your fingers
I danced

you dipped your hands
I bowed

you swayed to and fro
I leaped and soared

I moved as you directed
and obeyed every command

but now

I have decided

to sever these strings

and direct my own actions

my first steps

will be wobbly
and unsure

however

I would rather fall limp
to the stage

than be controlled by you
any longer

I will wait
for another Marionette

with whom I can sing
and dance
and love

no strings attached

Lament for Humanity

Humanity! Humanity!
O wretched flesh and bone
The frailty of the wounded heart
The tears which fall alone

O life, so fraught with suffering
That overwhelms our souls
What paradise eludes our grasp?
Where lay the sacred scrolls?

Humanity! Humanity!
So steeped in grief and woe
Like Icarus who plummeted
To distant earth below

Does Eden's holy tree still bloom?
Do dreams and visions call?
We strive to gain the Promised Land
Yet reach the Wailing Wall

O storm-tossed seas on which we sail
How strong thy currents flow
Poseidon claims the wreckage from
Thy churning undertow

Humanity! Humanity!
How great thy anguished cries
So hard some days to persevere
So hard some days to rise

I mourn for thee, Humanity!
And for myself as well
Enshackled by mortality
In Time's eternal cell

Nature's Symphony

A symphony of nature plays each night outside my door
An operatic serenade whose movements I adore
It's joined by graceful dancers who perform their lithe ballet
A theater of worship at the ending of each day

I sit in rapt enthrallment through the charmed melodious eve
Attentive to the rhythmic tunes and harmonies they weave
Their overture starts slowly as participants arrive
To join a grassroots orchestra which slowly comes alive

Each evenfall performer has a part within this show
The bobbing of the fireflies who cast an amber glow
The flitting of the hummingbird which weaves its fickle flight
The darting of the blackbird through the velvet of the night

The lumb'ring of the June bug as it drones above the ground
The hooting of a spotted owl which echoes all around
The croaking of the bullfrog with his baritone refrain
The trilling pulse of crickets from their camouflaged domain

The consummate Conductor leads this grand symphonic play
And oversees each terpsichorean coda and Bourrée
These canticles and anthems cast a calming spell so deep
Which soothe my restless spirit as my mind drifts off in sleep

Lost

That day you set sail was a day I lament
A day of misfortune no words could prevent
I begged you to stay but you chose to depart
Your ship left the dock while still moored to my heart

For several long nights I remained on that pier
In hopes that your bow might once more reappear
Then after a time I was forced to concede
Those dreams that I harbored would only recede

I chartered a vessel and plotted a course
Pursuing your love through the wakes of remorse
Through turbulent waters and ominous swells
My thoughts were consumed by those final farewells

I travelled the route I believed you had sailed
Yet contrary currents and harsh winds prevailed
The sea spray would moisten my face at the wheel
Disguising those tears that I fought to conceal

My vacant eyes stared toward the dull listless sky
Reliving the joys of those seaports gone by
My heart hammered judgment as if to proclaim
My ruinous pride bears the brunt of the blame

I'm so lost without you, the nights never end
The days ring so hollow, it's hard to pretend
Your memory haunts me through cloud covered days
Like phantoms that glide through the gray misty haze

~

A tempest is brewing with furious gales
The wind pelts my face and has ruptured the sails
My vessel is tossed and maneuvers no more
It cries for your beacon to guide me towards shore

The deck fills with water as storms take their toll
The stern has been damaged, I've lost all control
The masthead is cracked and the timbers all groan
My crewmen desert me, I'm left all alone

The tides overwhelm me and batter the keel
Like buffeting heartaches refusing to heal
I'm swept from the bridge into Neptune's abyss
A darkness devoid of your life-giving kiss

I swim for the wreckage that once was my boat
In desperate hopes of remaining afloat
I cling to the flotsam as if to your love
And offer my prayers to the heavens above

I'm shipwrecked without you, awash on the sand
Discarded like driftwood on desolate land
No traces remain of the vessel I sailed
Confirming the fact that my efforts have failed

I'll dwell on this island and dream of the day
You'll answer my call and transport me away
Yet should you not come in your seafaring ships
I'll go to my grave with your name on my lips

65

Alternate Realities

In alternate realities I hold you in my arms
Enraptured by your tenderness and captivating charms
I whisper secret covenants which fan love's smold'ring flame
And revel in the thought our lives will never be the same

In parallel dimensions we conclude our masquerade
And join the ballroom dancers in a formal promenade
We waltz to strains of melodies which cause our hearts to soar
Rejoicing in the knowledge that we'll be apart no more

In quadrants of the multiverse, my fondest hopes come true
To lie in floral meadows under crystal skies with you
We watch majestic billows as the clouds go gliding by
You kiss away the tears of joy which well up in my eyes

I've found that, over time and space, mere dreams don't satisfy
No matter which dimensions or domains they occupy
I've tossed aside the shackles that had bound my points of view
Pursuing astral visions 'til my cosmic my dreams come true

Listening Ear

All I can do is to sit by your side
And let you unburden your soul
All of my wisdom eludes me tonight
While wishing to ease and console

All I can offer is comfort and calm
A port for your ship in this storm
Answers to questions are not mine to give
I have just one task to perform

Speak to me now of your heartache and tears
Of trials and pain, old and new
Sharing your sorrows, I'll grant you an ear
And stay here all night 'til you're through

Lucid/Dream
(*For my father*)

Unto this day, I'm still not sure exactly what transpired
Perhaps my inner consciousness and fantasy conspired
Or maybe I was swept up in a dream-like state of mind
An altered state of cognizance that cannot be defined

The only thing I'm certain of was driving through a mist
An interstate anomaly I thought should not exist
The skies had been translucent in the moments just before
But then a fog descended like the sea upon a shore

I drove on through expecting it to dissipate and clear
A transient opaqueness that would quickly disappear
Yet when it did I saw a sight that could not be denied
My dearly missed and long-departed father by my side

I should have been incredulous and shocked by what I saw
But felt instead a mixture of contentment laced with awe
Now clarity eludes me as I recollect that scene
Not slumbering or wakeful, but some threshold in between

I only know I drove on towards a distant ray of light
Upon that desert road without another car in sight
And with my father seated there, I had so much to say
So calmly, I accepted this reunion underway

I started with apologies for thoughtless words expressed
In times of brash rebellion, hiding secrets unconfessed
I should have been more open, yet I chose to not confide
I robbed myself of wisdom from the answers he'd provide

I also asked forgiveness for not seeking his advice
Which, lacking in discernment, cost me much too high a price
A treasure trove of knowledge and perspective was at hand
If only I'd been teachable and prone to understand

"I know that it was me who grew apart and pulled away
While you were always steadfast in the love that you'd display
The consequence is hard to bear, much more since you've been gone
I oft succumb to guilt which leaves me sullen and withdrawn"

But then, to change the subject to a lighter frame of mind,
I spoke about his legacy of grandkids left behind
The ones he never got to see and children that they sired
The trouble they got into and the mayhem that transpired

I shared our genealogy, my passions and career
It made pause and wonder; should I cease or persevere
But still, he sat there smiling as if wanting to hear more
And so I kept on talking like I never had before

I poured my soul out freely as my spirit felt relief
Those times of faith and courage, those of doubt and unbelief
I seemed to sense the time we shared would very soon conclude
Upon this desert highway in this mystic interlude

The ray of light I'd traveled toward grew brighter as I neared
And also seemed more sizable than when it first appeared
Then suddenly it filled the air; I found myself immersed
Engulfed within its brilliance as a portal was traversed

And when the light abated from that luminous ordeal
I found myself at home alone, still seated at the wheel
I sat there for the longest time, afraid to break the spell
My heart and mind revolving like a rampant carousel

So now, I sit awake some nights and wonder, was it real?
A jackpot prize I garnered from some cosmic roulette wheel?
A ghostly visitation from the realms that lie beyond?
A guilty conscience yearning for a chance to correspond?

I know I'll never ascertain the truth about that ride
The answers that I long for may be evermore denied
And yet, I've found a comfort that I cannot quite convey
In telling dad those words I never found the time to say

In All My Dreams

In all my dreams I'm searching yet I'm never sure what for
Attracted by a siren song whose strains I can't ignore
It stirs a strange expectancy that burns within my chest
And spurs me on an odyssey to quell my deep unrest

In all my dreams I'm striving to attain some unknown goal
Yet many times rejection and frustration take their toll
I wish to savor triumph and exult in sweet success
To persevere with honor and refuse to acquiesce

In all my dreams I play a part within a scripted scene
Like actors in a silent film upon the silver screen
At times, I'm inattentive to the set director's cues
Distracted by the drama of my melancholy muse

In all my dreams lie obstacles I seek to overcome
And yet I fear too frequently my heart and I succumb
I long to cross this Rubicon and see what lands await
Perhaps to solve the riddle of my enigmatic fate

I wonder if these dreams are mere illusions of the mind
Or if they harbor secrets for my consciousness to find
I've always been a dreamer from the time that I was small
But lately I'm not sure these dreams mean anything at all

The Anguished Heart

(on the death of my beautiful son, Jon)

"Betrayed", the anguished heart cries out
In wounded grief from love devout
Till morning, beats its sorrowed tune
Beneath a cold uncaring moon

The plaintive sobs awash with tears,
Lamenting groans that no one hears
Resound within the bedroom walls
And echoes faint through empty halls

The tortured soul can scarce find rest
Within a pained and heavy chest
The sleepless eyes cannot recite
The poems sweet which youth didst write

What cruel injustice thrusts its spear
Through gentle life and love sincere?
What wind unrighteous blows so cold
On kindness graced by virtue bold?

O peace, thy absent voice I miss
Forsaken in this dark abyss
O comfort, in thy warm embrace
I long to hide my tear-stained face

"Betrayed", the wounded heart cries out
With broken faith and waves of doubt
Till evening, sounds a weary knell
Desiring not to say 'farewell'

Parting

If parting's such sweet sorrow
When do sorrow's waves subside
And yield their flow to sweetness
As the changing of the tide

When minutes seem like hours
And each day is like a year
Then night becomes eternity
Through which we persevere

If parting's such sweet sorrow
Born of love's exquisite pain
I'll savor not that sweetness
'Til I hold you once again

How shall I describe her

Yet how shall I describe her when mere words will not suffice
With language such a shallow and inadequate device
To venture such a task is to embark upon a quest
With naught but scant provisions and a burning in my breast

Her eyes are like two islands in a placid sea remote
Her voice is like a sonnet fair that Shakespeare's pen once wrote
Her heartbeat softly echoes through the rhythm of the night
Her smile ignites the eastern sky which heralds dawn's first light

Her footsteps fall so graceful like an elegant ballet
Her laughter rings like church bells when they peal on Christmas day
Her passionate embraces bring my weary soul such cheer
Her lips impart such ecstasy, I tremble drawing near

The brightness of her countenance dispels my darkest mood
The traces of her fragrance flood my soul with hopes renewed
My tongue cannot begin to voice the happiness she brings
Nor comprehend the boundless depths of love from whence it springs

Once upon a time

I once believed in fairy tales
And fables old and new
When wishing on an ev'ning star
Could make my dreams come true

My young imagination
Would delight in all I'd read
Of kings and queens and castles
Or a knight's heroic deed

I'd sit entranced for hours
By the spell my books would weave
Of realms beyond the rainbow
In the land of make believe

But now those childhood reveries
Have vanished with the breeze
They've long since been supplanted
By responsibilities

I wonder if the things I've gained
Outweigh the ones I've lost
Or if my life's attainments
Came at far too high a cost

At times I try to recollect
The wonder that I'd feel
When life was full of magic
And my fantasies seemed real

I wish I could recapture
All the joyfulness sublime
The rapture and the innocence
Of 'once upon a time'

Untitled

I'd rather have respect than love
Integrity than fame
I'd rather live with honor
Than to bear a tainted name

I care not for preeminence
Prestige or glory's crown
For all those who exalt themselves
Will one day be brought down

Love's Passing

I mourned love's passing through the night
And sought its swift return
I wandered barren country sides
Where grows the bristle fern

I mourned with bitter tears of grief
Near streams of scarlet sage
And saw reflected in that flow
The passing of an age

With heavy heart I stood and watched
From lofty tower heights
The evening skies were set ablaze
As passion's torch burned bright

Yet then I stopped and pondered on
Those days that did enthrall
'Twas nectar sweet that crossed my lips
Its taste I still recall

Like combs from whence the honey drips
Those mem'ries still afford
A stream in which to quench my thirst
And savor love's reward

Yea, love no longer roams these hills
Nor beckons from yon knoll
Yet lingers still its fragrant scent
Within my windswept soul

Escape

I wish to take my leave of life's
encumbrances and cares
for just a while, to circumvent
the weight of its affairs

I do not ask to be removed
from daily joys and trials
but only to escape a bit
to some secluded isles

Or maybe some remote locale
where no one knows my name
and abdicate my station in
this enterprising game

A respite from the vast concerns
and burdens of this earth
a time of contemplation or
a spiritual rebirth

I only need some place to just
refresh my weary soul
a sea on which to drift away
a beach on which to stroll

I'd then return to face the world
with confidence renewed
a fresh and cheerful state of mind
a readjusted mood

Ocean of Tears

Part I: The Storm
Above the wind-tossed troubled seas
A vessel pitched and yawed
The name it bore: "The Clarion"
From ports that lay abroad

As Captain Lucas manned the helm
He spied a distant shore
An island off the starboard bow
Beyond the torrent's roar

He struggled through the turbulent
Tempestuous marine
While deep below those wind-tossed waves
Aurora swam unseen

Part II: Aurora
She slipped through hidden currents like
A seagull through the skies
With long cascading mermaid hair
And sparkling turquoise eyes

She traced the captain's passage through
Her oceanic sphere
A world of breathless majesty
A limitless frontier

She followed towards the coral reef
Wherein his voyage stopped
The sails were furled and stowed away
The massive anchored dropped

Part III: Lucas
He loved to walk the deck at night
And breathe the salty air
Survey the constellations
And recite his evening prayer

The ocean felt like home to him
The tides, his lover's arms
The breeze, a long-impassioned kiss
With soft beguiling charms

He longed to satisfy his thirst
To venture and explore
Uncover secrets long submerged
Along the ocean floor

Part IV: Aurora
She'd often float above the waves
And watch the seagulls glide
Unfettered from their earthly bonds
A joy, for her, denied

She loved the ocean's freedom yet
At times, she felt confined
For fleeting are the days
When you're the last one of your kind

She longed to be unshackled
From her watery domain
Explore the topographic world
Where shoreline meets terrain

Part V: The Island
The crew and shipmates disembarked
And fought their way ashore
To wait until the storm had passed
And seas were calm once more

They fashioned crude encampments
Using tarp and canvass tents
While Lucas, to secure their site,
Began reconnaissance

He came upon a hidden cove
An inlet ringed by rocks
And found himself confronted with
A living paradox

Part V: Aurora and Lucas
She lay upon a rocky shelf
Protruding from the sea
Her face conveyed no fearfulness
Just curiosity

She'd oft explored those sunken ships
Destroyed before their time
The briny decomposed remains
Of sailors in their prime

Yet never had she met before
A human face to face
A living incarnation from
The surface-dwelling race

~

He'd heard the stories sailors tell
In pubs at every port
Of Sirens and monstrosities
And beasts of every sort

Some swore they'd witnessed angels
While still others, demon spawn
Yet Lucas rarely paid them heed
And let them ramble on

He'd seen his share of oddities
Which gave him pause to think
Yet mostly just concluded that
They'd had too much to drink

Part VI: The Cove

They gazed upon each other
Through the pouring sheets of rain
Both filled with strange emotions
Neither one could ascertain

A seagull circled overhead
The waves still crashed and swelled
Enchantment seemed to fill the cove
Mystique unparalleled

No sounds nor words did either speak
Their eyes conveyed it all
For eyes surpass the spoken word
And scale the highest wall

How long they both remained there,
Neither one could truly tell
They barely dared to move or breathe
Afraid to break the spell

Then came a crewman's shout nearby
Reporting on their plight
Aurora slipped into the cove
And disappeared from sight

Part VII: Repairs

For several days the crew had worked
Repairing masts and sails
And each day Lucas stole away
Down hidden well-worn trails

They met as much as time allowed
And very soon, embraced
Two lost and lonely kindred souls
Their hearts now interlaced

He loved her eyes, her lips, her hair
The fragrant smells thereof
She loved the way he held her as
The seagull soared above

Part VIII: Departure
Then came the day that Lucas feared
'Twas time to man his helm
For neither one could coexist
Within the others' realm

He had a duty to his ship
His country and his men
Such things, Aurora could not grasp
Nor fully comprehend

And yet, she knew within her heart
The path that fate decreed
Her love for him was such, she had
No choice but to accede

She could not live upon the land
Nor he, within the sea
They both had little choice but to
Accept reality

Part IX: Ocean of Tears
The ship set out for open seas
The first mate at the wheel
For though a ship can be repaired
The heart is not soon healed

And in the Captain's quarters
Lucas wept with great dismay
Aurora cried unceasingly
The seagull flew away

Untitled

The Oaks stretch forth their canopy
Caressing heaven's face
While eagles' wings brush mountain crests
Which time cannot erase

The rivers wind through woodland paths
Where finches flit and dart
Yet all is vain and worthless if
I cannot touch your heart

Meeting Again (for the first time)

I met her again for the first time
A legion of seasons had passed
The years had swept over and through us
A mountain of dies had been cast

I found her familiar yet different
Unknown and yet strangely the same
The contrast between who we once were
And who, over time, we became

Commencing with pleasant exchanges
We cautiously shared and inquired
Of life's many pleasures and triumphs
And tragic events that transpired

We spoke of decisions and choices
Some inconsequential and moot
Yet others with ramifications
From poorly sown seeds that bore fruit

Our dialogue weaved and meandered
O'er topics both weighty and small
Conversing on matters of substance
And other times, nothing at all

The sheltering sky stretched above us
A vast panorama of blue
It seemed to induce reminiscing
On all of the things we'd been through

We drank from the cup of nostalgia
And toasted the forthcoming years
Lamenting how days pass so quickly
And how fast our youth disappears

We walked by the banks of the river
Where currents and sentiments flowed
Their rhythm in tune to our heartbeat
Affections so richly bestowed

While strolling past fountains and gardens
Emotions, long dormant, emerged
The wind shifted ever so slightly
The past and the present converged

Near bridges of dreams, I embraced her
On boardwalks of cedar, we kissed
My thoughts spanned the years and reflected
On past opportunities missed

The sidewalks were bustling with people
The young and the old passing by
Yet, standing there nestled together,
It felt there were just her and I

I treasure that day by the river
And later, our walks in the park
The intimate moments together
Her whispering voice in the dark

Another Day (without you)

Another day passes mundanely
The tedious minutes accrue
The hours drag sluggishly forward
Another day spent without you

My mind cannot cease from its mulling
Nor pondering bygone affairs
In hopes of elusive discernment
And answers to myriad prayers

I cannot say plainly for certain
Exactly what missteps were made
Which led to your sudden departure
A scene that I've often replayed

What words were omitted or spoken
To cause this precipitous loss
Perhaps there were subtleties present
Whose substance did not come across

Perchance my reserved disposition
Was seen as too distant and cold
Although hidden passions burn brightest
They're seldom effusive or bold

I've written you dozens of missives
Discarding each one in a heap
For words are an awkward contrivance
And can't convey stirrings this deep

Another night listlessly passes
My thoughts toss with restless unease
I've wrestled, at times, with emotions
But never with ones such as these

Affliction

(Dedicated to poets past)

Such beauty flows from artists
Whose creative flames are fanned
By winds of harsh discouragement
Or hardship's calloused hand

Such keen discerning insights
Are entrusted to the care
Of those whose fragile spirits
Have endured life's grievous snares

Such deep impassioned verses
Which are writ by candle's glow
Are paid in full by sufferings
This world so oft bestows

Imprints

I sometimes sit and ponder on the role our senses play
In capturing the imagery which permeates each day
The sights that dance before our eyes and sounds that greet our ears
All seep into our consciousness, then slumber there for years

These opulent impressions, when combined with touch and smell,
Comprise a magic storehouse where the ghosts of yore still dwell
The richness of emotions that these imprints all contain
Are like the lush and fertile fields which grace some distant plain

They're tinged with subtle textures like a palette's shades and hues
Adorned with moods and feelings that we never seem to lose
The meanings and significance these memories impart
Can only be interpreted within our secret heart

They lie untouched for ages in the realms of 'where' and 'when'
Yet in a poignant moment they can spring to life again
It's more than recollection of events from long ago
And stronger than remembrances of those we used to know

It's like a fresh immersion in the pools of yesterday
Enveloped by sensations that no language can convey
You find yourself transported to a moment from your past
Awash with thoughts and sentiments so tangible and vast

It may have been a romance or a lover's last farewell
A weekend at a cottage bathed in nature's tranquil spell
It's sometimes sadly bittersweet or comforting and calm
The pang of melancholy or a gentle soothing balm

The triggers for these episodes are varied and unique
A moment in the moonlight touched by twilight's deep mystique
An image in a photograph, the fragrance of perfume
The passionate aroma of a honeysuckle's bloom

But sometimes it's the hearing of a long-forgotten song
That stirs those ancient wellsprings with an undertow so strong
The veil between the 'new' and 'old' evaporates like dew
Removing all distinctions that can separate the two

These imprints are mysterious in ways we can't explain
The secrets of their timelessness, we'll never ascertain
From depths of unawareness to the forefront of our mind
At unexpected moments, 'now' and 'then' become entwined

Battleground

And so goes the conflict that rages
Incessantly fought through the years
A battle that rings through the ages
And spreads across distant frontiers

The tide of this war often changes
From smoldering darkness to light
Yet, cursing the shame of my weakness,
I ofttimes relinquish my fight

The ghosts of remorse dance before me
Parading misdeeds from my past
They dredge through the muck and the mire
For cruel accusations to cast

I grovel in abject surrender
Acknowledging guilt and regret
My hollow excuses are worthless
I cannot escape nor forget

Then angels of mercy console me
Resplendent in raiment of white
They speak of a mighty Crusader
Who rescues the poor and contrite

A Paladin conquering hero
Who one day will make all things right
They bid me accept His protection
And savor His kingdom's delight

I struggle to understand pardon
When judgment is what I deserve
My life has been selfish and wicked
And not worth the price to preserve

Still, freedom is what I consent to
Affirming the choice that I make
An heir to a kingdom of glory
Of which I will one day partake

Yet on goes the battle that rages
Whose ending seems sometimes unsure
And though I may stumble and falter
My future at last is secure

Tender Moments

I love those tender moments when my heart reclines with yours
Like drifting on a placid sea beyond Sorrento's shores
Such peace I seldom savor in a world of strife and woe
Enraptured by the ecstasy your arms and lips bestow

Those precious times our spirits touch recapture Eden's bliss
Where paradise unveils its joys with each impassioned kiss
The daily cares and burdens of this life all melt away
Supplanted by the soothing balm your tranquil eyes convey

I love those tender moments which I pray will never cease
Those cherished quiet interludes that grant me sweet release
The fragrance of your perfume as your head lies on my chest
Relieves my mind of conflicts and allays my soul's unrest

The Gulf

When words fall through the crevices of logic's flawed design
And lie in knotted tangles like an aimless creeping vine
The inconsistent rationales are bared for all to see
Amidst the smold'ring ashes of discordance's debris

When poems fail to touch the soul and rhymes do not appear
When prose no longer resonates nor cadence persevere
The tattered threads of orphaned verses litter barren floors
In disillusioned apathy which consonance ignores

When tears replace the empty space where dialogue once flowed
When silence fills the garden paths where love was once bestowed
Then nature's charms no longer calm nor soothe the troubled soul
But linger as reminders of enchanted ev'ning strolls

When reason's course seems plainly clear yet contradicts the heart
What wisdom can we trust in when the two are worlds apart?
No remedy seems viable to bridge the endless span
That stretches like a gulf between a woman and a man

Death Stops By
(Inspired by Emily Dickenson)

When Death stopped by for coffee
We sat beneath an oak
Our conversation lingered
On life's unwieldy yoke

I asked him why our summers
Advance at first too slow
Then gather steam so quickly
The further that we go

I asked him why we struggle
When life should be so sweet
And wondered why our efforts
So often face defeat

He listened to my questions
And nodded as I spoke
I searched his eyes for answers
Beneath his hooded cloak

He understood these problems
Much better than the rest
Yet spoke he not a whisper
To answer my request

We savored lemon muffins
And fresh banana bread
Our teacups brimmed with coffee
While birds flew overhead

I asked why people feared him
Since one day, all will fade
From sweeping golden wheat fields
To tender sun-kissed glades

I questioned him on fairness
And how he makes his choice
Between the heartless tyrant
And one who has no voice

Then Death reached for his napkin
And dabbed his ashen lips
His face was like a tombstone
Beneath a cold eclipse

The August sky turned sullen
As Death and I arose
Our coffee time was over
Forever, I suppose

His arm around my shoulder,
We ventured toward the road
I knew this path would lead me
Unto my new abode

Yet as we walked, I listened
And heard Death speak my name
He answered all my questions
And fanned my wond'ring flame

The plan, I saw quite clearly
Which satisfied my thirst
No longer need I question
With knowledge now disbursed

And back beneath the oak tree
Our bread was caked with mold
The ants had swarmed the muffins
The coffee had turned cold

A Lover's Return

(An ode to spring)

At last, my love, I see thy face
Returning o'er yon hill
Thy welcome smile ignites the glen
And brings my soul a thrill

When last I saw thee from afar
Thy countenance had changed
The passion of our deep romance
Had somehow turned estranged

Thine absence lo these many months
Hath left me in distress
I've mourned thee with an aching heart
Which words cannot express

But now the dark has turned to dawn
And mourning to delight
As dormant yearnings spring to life
Within yon breaking light

I thought that I had loved thee

I thought that I had loved thee
Through these long impassioned days
'Twas mere infatuation
With the kindness of your ways

I loved our conversations
Midst the leisure of our strolls
Thy words were balm and ointment
As I bared my troubled soul

Thy hand clasped mine so freely
As our fingers interlaced
It gave me strength and comfort
Through the trials that I faced

Yet as the season ended
Many thoughts were left unsaid
It pained me sore to wonder
If my heart had been misled

I thought that I had loved thee
Through the summer's serenade
Your eyes conveyed confusion
As my love began to fade

For Naught

The tempter passed my dwelling in the fading light of day
And turned his eye upon me as a lion to its prey
He whispered of my failings and lay bare my old regrets
While ridiculing comforts that a simple life begets

Then smote he all the pleasures that my humble life did yield
From recompense of toilings to the reapings of my field
Yet still, his anger smoldered at the lack of his success
For through these cruel afflictions I succumbed not to distress

Then spake I to this enemy of all that's good and kind
This adversary steeped in hate who seeks to rob and bind
My words betrayed my weariness yet held a sense of peace
That caused my foe to falter and his harsh assaults to cease

"For naught, thy winds assail my keep and arrows pierce my soul
So let thy mighty torrents strike and tempests take their toll
The One who lives and died for me hath claimed me as his own
So all my days upon this earth are His and His alone"

Look past these words

Look past these stoic words, I pray
Of shallow form which lead astray
And delve beyond their rigid cast
To realms of beauty unsurpassed

O look not on each steadfast verse
But in their hidden depths immerse
For words can naught but point the way
Toward realms removed where dreams hold sway

Be not deceived by simple prose
Concealing tides and undertows
But lift your ears toward distant strains
Of wayward ships and lonely trains

I pray thee, search beyond the page
For echoes from a bygone age
And savor scenes where lovers swoon
'neath Grecian skies and Cyprus moon

The measured rhyme can ne'er convey
The pangs of romance gone astray
Nor kindle flames in love's abode
Where whispered vows were once bestowed

Ships and Islands
(*on loneliness and the hopes of romance*)

I've lived upon this desert isle alone for many years
Some days are uneventful so they fade and disappear
On other days I'm occupied by some ambitious quest
To chase away the tedium and calm my restlessness

I search for hidden trinkets in the secret island caves
Although the items found within are not the ones I crave
Within my heart there stirs a discontent that won't subside
Which longs for something greater than this island can provide

Each day I sit upon the shore and watch the ships pass by
Their smokestacks trailing distant wisps across the aqua sky
They drift so calm and full of grace in mute tranquility
Beyond the faint horizon at the point of mystery

Some days a mist surrounds them and conceals them from my sight
And other days acuity reveals their vast delights
I yearn in vain for visits from these grand sea-faring hosts
Beyond my reach they travel, never drawing near my coasts

The seagulls cry above my head, the sand crabs dance and play
The dolphins off the coral reef perform their deft ballet
Yet all I hear are echoes from a far-off jubilee
And wonder if those cabin lights will one day come for me

I once discovered wreckage from a tempest-ravaged boat
And wondered how those gorgeous ships could fail to stay afloat
I thought about the risks involved in leaving safety's shore
Yet, in the end, concluded that they stood to gain much more

One day, with reckless disregard, I braved the daunting sea
And vowed to persevere until I reached my destiny
Yet late that night my hopes and I were washed upon the sand
My passions spent in conflict 'gainst the ocean's mighty hand

100

And so, each day I stroll the beach collecting coral shells
Constructing wreaths to decorate this island where I dwell
At night I lie upon my bed and watch the shadows play
Their ghostly drama tracing scenes in hues of ashen grey

I've built my fires each starlit night and raised a flag each dawn
But now, so many years have passed my hopes are all but gone
It's clear to me that some are born to sail in majesty
While others spend their days alone like islands in the sea

End of the Day

The day unwinds and deepens
At its slow and steady pace
The shadows stretch their tendrils
'cross the earth's expansive face

The sun retreats in silence
Towards its refuge o'er the dale
Receding from the vacant sky
As evening draws its veil

While dusk supplants the fading light
Whose sovereignty now ends
The blues and reds succumb to grays
As quietude descends

Then flowing sable tides of night
Wash o'er the twilight haze
And wipe away the vestiges
Of countless yesterdays

Traces

fingers tracing

outlines
of your name

obsidian etchings
'neath interlacing
snow-tinged branches

framed against
overcast shrouds

diffusing half-hearted light

memories bridging

the chasm of years

mystic junctions
where past and present converge

poems revealing
sweet fragrances of youth

like incense
forever sanctifying

your empty room

Former Residence

The doormat at the entrance still lies firmly in its place
With imprints of "I'm sorry" woven deeply through its face
Both hinges of the screen door dangle loosely on their frame
From years of being slammed about in fits of guilt and shame

This bleak and former residence, where once I used to live,
Was where my heart and soul were drained of all I had to give
This house has long stood vacant on the street I left behind
A dark forsaken neighborhood, to where it's now consigned

The peeling paint reflects that awful barrenness of doubt
And gardens of self-confidence lay desolate from drought
The shutters on the windows hang in broken disrepair
From winds of harsh discouragement and storms of grim despair

The floors are scuffed so carelessly where others used to tread
Not caring who they stepped on in their haste to get ahead
And cobwebs of duplicity hang draped throughout the room
Replacing hopes of romance with despondency and gloom

The cellar houses storage crates besmeared by dust and soot
Containing raw emotions coldly trampled underfoot
The dumpsters in the alleyway are heaped with gross abuse
Atop old sensitivities, which serve no further use

I left this former residence and vowed to not return
Except to pause and contemplate those lessons that I've learned
The ghosts I left behind here, I will never resurrect
For now they've been supplanted by esteem and self-respect

Time

There used to be a time when time was seldom on my mind
Unworthy of my interest or concern of any kind
But now it seems I think about it more and more each day
While contemplating ways in which its sovereignty holds sway

Its vague elusive nature is obscured in veiled mystique
Defying all attempts to grasp those answers that we seek
While some may find it fanciful, intrigued by time's effect,
Still others dread this nexus from which none can disconnect

I often make the argument that time is not our friend
It dominates our lives in ways we barely comprehend
I've seen too many casualties of time's unyielding reign
The loss of pride and dignity when comfort cedes to pain

They say 'with age comes wisdom' and I don't dispute that truth
Yet such a prize we forfeit by relinquishing our youth
I wonder who among us would not rather choose to stay
And sample simple pleasures of a single bygone day

I'm grateful for our memories, those wisps of past events
Which linger sweet as perfume with their gentle fragrant scents
While some are tinged with sadness there are many filled with joy
Instilling in us hopes that even time cannot destroy

Still, through the countless ages, flows this river towards the bend
A firm unchanging constant which appears to have no end
Though some may rail in anger or capitulate in fear
The measure of humanity is how we persevere

Cabin on the Lake

The solitude I savor in my cabin on the lake
Provides creative imagery of which I oft partake
The poems I compose here and the novels that I write
All fill the shelves of bookstores, to my editor's delight

My simple sparse surroundings serve to render all I need
By cultivating visions from a small yet fertile seed
These fully bloomed impressions then become my written prose
Enabling my life alone within this sweet repose

I listen through the morning mist as nature comes alive
The splashing of the herons as their daily flocks arrive
Across the lake I spy a pair of grazing antlered moose
While close nearby there strolls alone a honking long necked goose

As daylight sweeps across the lake I hear the osprey's song
A school of lake trout leap in play while mallards drift along
The sunlight brightly sparkles on the water's tranquil face
And bathes the woods in rapture like a lover's warm embrace

In evening as the sun departs, the darkness fills with sounds
Of prowling wolves and snapping twigs which echo all around
I see their tracks each morning just outside my cabin door
Reflecting scenes of hunted prey played out the night before

I need no more companionship than what this lake supplies
Its richness and tranquility is heaven in my eyes
I haven't any yearnings to go back from where I came
Where all my views were compromised in quests to find my fame

I've left that world of selfish deeds and words no man can trust
Where innocence was sacrificed for gains of the unjust
The life I live within these woods is one I'll not forsake
For mansions hold no beauty like my cabin on the lake

The Poet

The poet weaves his tales which speak
of love's undaunted quest
And pens impassioned verses which
arouse the lovelorn breast

His works describe those golden heights
which many yearn to scale
And renders but a fleeting glimpse
behind that sacred veil

Yet he, who writes of love's allure,
has never touched her face
Nor slept within that sweet abode
enveloped by her grace

For him, the words that fill his page
describe a foreign land
Which vibrates with exotic tongues
he longs to understand

He pines for love's insistent call
to feel its fervent ache
Yet fears this holy pilgrimage
is one he'll never take

Each night his musings turn to realms
he hungers to traverse
He wipes aside a wayward tear
And pens another verse

Moment in Time

If life could grant a single day
To hold for evermore
A sliver of infinity
From time's eternal shore

I'd choose that placid August morn
Beneath cerulean skies
Where once I held you in my arms
And gazed into your eyes

Betrayal

When truth is discarded and trust is obscure
Our faith in humanity fights to endure
When stripes are inflicted which linger and burn
The twice-stricken cheek is not easy to turn

I wonder why people resort to deceit?
To nurture their pride or to feed their conceit?
Some wounds that we suffer take longer to mend
A knife cuts much deeper when held by a friend

Timeless Love

He always knew he'd find her in that city by the bay
Where vast suspension bridges loom and coastal waters sway
He made his way from Texas during Nineteen ninety-eight
As dreams of love's fulfillment beckoned from a westward state

They called him with a promise of the one he yearned to meet
The woman of his visions who would make his life complete
He came to San Francisco with its rolling hills and roads
He loved the ocean fragrance when the tepid waters flowed

He wandered through the city from South Beach to Lincoln Park
Then settled on a region where he sensed her timeless spark

~

She always knew she'd find him where the land gave way to sea
Near foggy bays and coves is where her heart said he would be
She traveled there from Utah where she'd just turned twenty-two
Compelled to find the destiny she knew she must pursue

She marveled at this city and the sights when she arrived
Amazed by its recovery, in awe of how it thrived
The coming Exposition near the famous Golden Gate
Would soon attract the masses as they journeyed to that strait

Perhaps he'd be among those who would come to see the Fair
A kind and thoughtful traveler in answer to her prayer
She found a private area for what she had in mind
Her spirit knew she'd find him through a test that she'd designed

She first removed her locket with a photograph enclosed
Then wrapped it in her kerchief so as not to be exposed
She dug a hole and buried it beneath a willow's shade
Then kissed the earth so gently where her hopes and dreams were laid

~

110

Each day he'd wait with patience as he watched the passers by
Convinced he'd recognize her once his gaze would catch her eye
One day, quite absentmindedly, while resting on the ground
He took a twig and dug a hole surprised by what he found

He slowly cleared the dirt away to view the prize within
A simple modest heirloom from the spot where she had been
He gazed upon the picture stored so lovingly inside
And knew he'd finally found her as he stood and softly cried

~

He held her locket tightly near the great Pacific shore
Exactly where she'd buried it just sixty years before

O Cursed Pen

O wretched poet that I be
A madman tossed on Melville's sea
A windmill from Cervante's myth
Which Don Quixote struck forthwith

O woeful prose of harsh travails
The worst of times from Dickens' tales
A shipwreck in Defoe's vast tome
Or Lovecraft's musty catacomb

O rhymes that do not sing or dance
Like Shakespeare's plays of lost romance
A tell-tale heart from Poe's dark verse
Which whispers of a family curse

O lines of pain and great despair
Like mortals in Medusa's lair
Or worldly wars and tolling bells
From Hemmingway and Herbert Wells

O cursed pen that fails the page
A victim of this modern age
I mourn the truth that, from my pen,
Flow not the words of greater men

Dreams

So dreams are just for dreaming and are better left in bed
To seep into the pillowcase on which I'd laid my head
They're better left entangled in the patterns of my sheets
Discarded in the morning's light, disheveled at my feet

They can't survive the daylight or the world outside my door
Where dreams confront reality like waves against the shore
They only thrive at midnight when enchantment still holds sway
To dance amidst the moonlight like a faerie child at play

So dreams are just for dreaming, then evaporate at dawn
Their remnants float like ashes in the sunlight then they're gone
They leave behind an imprint which remains throughout the day
A residue of longing for each dream that slipped away

Read My Heart

When the spoken word forsakes me

And my faltering tongue fumbles with clumsy but well-intentioned expressions of my passion

When my awkward speech muddles each pure and noble thought that I labor to endow with breath

read my heart

When the written word eludes me

And my feeble attempts at poetic release lie in a crumpled reviled heap

When not even the august words of long-entombed poets adequately reflect the depths of emotions coursing through my soul

read my heart

114

When all reason deserts me

And my inexplicable actions expose me as one standing on the fringe of madness

When my fevered mind finds no shade in which to seek sanctuary

nor oasis in which to sojourn

during my nomadic quest to understand just how desperately I need you

…read my heart

Shades of Gray

I love those gray and shrouded days diffused with light subdued
A silky haze so indistinct it seems to mull and brood
A veiled and timeless essence which encompasses the land
And cradles our emotions deep within its sullen hand

I love that in-between time when it doesn't seem like day
Yet neither is it evening when the sovereign moon holds sway
It's like you've been transported to another realm in space
Where time has been suspended in an eerie cloaked embrace

A balmy breeze enfolds the air which whispers soft and low
With voices of a distant age within its tranquil flow
A time of hushed reflection on those thoughts that won't let go
Or bittersweet remembrances of romance long ago

I find myself adrift amidst enchantment of the eve
Where past and present coalesce and mem'ries interweave
I almost sense the presence of those loved ones left behind
Within this hour of mystery which captivates my mind

A tinge of melancholy with a touch of hope serene
A fragile time of visions when the ghosts of dusk convene
Those dreams we held as children or regrets we cannot quell
All mingle in this ambiance, cocooned within its spell

I can't convey the feelings that these magic days impart
Nor offer words of clarity on why they move my heart
Between the joy and suffering, beyond the light of day
There lies a quiet interlude within these shades of gray

116

April 19th

If only it were possible
To slow the heavens' pace
Or pause the earth's rotation
And suspend the stars in space

I'd anchor evening's mantle
So it held the dawn at bay
And do my best to circumvent
The coming of the day

Oasis

The desert stretches endlessly as far as eye can see
Throughout these arid regions like an undulating sea
I trek across the rippling sands in search of journey's end
Where lies a dream of happiness I hope to apprehend

The sun beats down relentlessly on those who dwell below
The sojourners and nomads as they travel to and fro
The lizards, snakes and scorpions that slither, creep and crawl
The meerkat and the camel as they heed the desert's call

At times the heat is bearable and slackens not my stride
At other times, unmerciful; refusing to subside
On days like these my throat is parched, my lips are chapped and raw
I long for fruit on which to sup, a well from which to draw

Your love is my oasis when the desert sandstorms swell
When tempests whip my weathered face with winds I cannot quell
You offer shade and sustenance, a respite from the gale
And cool my scorched and fevered mind 'til calmer winds prevail

I sometimes view mirages when the haze deceives my sight
I know they're just illusions from the blinding desert light
They make it hard to concentrate and focus on my quest
Diverting my attention from the goals towards which I've pressed

I've walked alone in silence with the eagle as my guide
I've ridden with the caravan across this great divide
I've learned to live on equal terms with sorrow and delight
And pondered life's enigmas in my Bedouin tent at night

I've seen the desert lightning flash amidst torrential rain
And witnessed bleached white skeletons that dot the bronze terrain
Discovered hidden waterfalls and bathed within their stream
And found that tribulations are not always what they seem

Your love is my oasis when I'm buffeted about
When hurts and wrongs I've suffered fill my mind with fear and doubt
You tend to my infirmities beneath the midnight skies
Then serenade my slumbers with exotic lullabies

A Blue Part of Town

When daylight surrenders to twilight's advance
My mind turns to mem'ries of bygone romance
I gaze out the window in pensive desire
My ghostly reflection inflamed by the fire

As thoughts overwhelm me of times we once knew
Emotions arise that I cannot subdue
In silent reflection, I head out the door
And saunter down streets where your foot falls no more

I visit that part of the town we once strolled
Where plans for our future would slowly unfold
With elegant splendor the moon weaves her spell
Unveiling those scenes I envision so well

The bench at the bus stop sits lonely and bare
Recalling the rides that we both used to share
We'd circle the city till street lamps awoke
Transforming the city as dusk drew her cloak

The storefronts seem vacant, where once they displayed
The latest in fashions, all brightly arrayed
I promised you one day I'd purchase them all
No matter the future or what might befall

The booths in the diner look empty and void
Yet still can I picture those times we enjoyed
We'd talk about nothing and laugh while we ate
Like starry-eyed teens on our very first date

The local museum no longer attracts
With Mesopotamia's staid artifacts
Those remnants of history only remind
Of passion's lost glory, forever enshrined

120

As raindrops descend from the cloud-laden skies
They mirror the tears welling up in my eyes
I turned up my collar and head further west
Down cracked asphalt streets where my soul finds no rest

The clicking of train tracks is heard from afar
As neon lights buzz over Sullivan's bar
The cross from the mission still shines through the night
Proclaiming its hope to the poor and contrite

The traffic lights blink in a soulless display
While casting strange shadows that flicker and sway
I splash through the puddles which rains have amassed
Their ripples reflecting old ghosts from the past

The sounds from the city diminish and wane
Like echoes of love I can never reclaim
My heart feels so empty, deserted and bare
It wanders the streets like a cab with no fare

I still can recall every color and hue
From days when I'd walk down these sidewalks with you
But now all the buildings seem lifeless and brown
Just haunted remains in a blue part of town

Soliloquy

The stage is bare and empty as I enter from the wings
While musing over subjects which pertain to many things
A vacant auditorium spreads out before my view
To which I'll share my troubled heart before this night is through

Preparing my delivery, I stand and clear my throat
My mind awash with famous bards and those whom I might quote
A solitary spotlight shines from rafters overhead
To highlight my soliloquy of things that must be said

"I have some topics on my mind I've wanted to address
And towards that goal I'll strive to be succinct and not digress
My statements may be commonplace and touch on nothing new
But maybe they'll remind us of another point of view

I'm tired of hurtful comments which so often cross our lips
And linger with abandon like a fleet of unmoored ships
It takes so little effort just to pause before we speak
To weigh our words more carefully or turn the other cheek

It's not a crime to differ with opinions that we hear
As long as our discussions stem from reason, not from fear
And is it so absurd to hope, or too much to expect,
That when we disagree we show a portion of respect

And speaking of respect, it seems that notion's all but dead
It's been replaced by snide remarks and caustic barbs instead
We criticize our youth bemoaning troubled seeds they've sown
Forgetting that their acts are mere reflections of our own

There was a time when honor meant much more to men than life
When love of God and country fueled our souls in times of strife
Yet now it seems we've tossed aside those precepts from the past
To substitute our heritage with creeds that will not last

I know that through the course of years we often change our mind
When stances that we've held may be discarded or refined
But certain truths are sacred and not subject to debate
You either hold them close or risk a fool's ignoble fate

There needs to be a line from which a man will not retreat
A place from which he'll stand and fight and even risk defeat
A cause that he'll contend for with his back against the wall
For he who stands for nothing falls for anything at all"

I briefly pause to take a drink and scan the barren hall
Uncertain if my spoken words mean anything at all
For just a passing moment, I consider turning back
Yet something moves me forward down this solitary track

"I find it not unseemly for a man to shed a tear
For innocents who suffer or for values he holds dear
Compassion, love and empathy are traits we should admire
And yet, for some, these attributes seem harder to acquire

If children are our future (which is what we once believed)
Then shouldn't we protect them from the time that they're conceived?
There is no greater tragedy for which our hearts should mourn
Than when our laws abandon them before they're even born

I still remember clearly when we used to pray in school
When teachers spoke of character and taught the Golden Rule
What happened to our patriots and those we once revered?
They've been replaced by counterfeits, exactly as I feared

My father taught me many things I try to not forget
Like not to be a victim and to work for what I get
Obey the Ten Commandments and encourage those in need
To not succumb to jealousy, resentment, lust or greed

He also used to tell me that my word should be my bond
To do my job with excellence and strive to go beyond
These precepts still are valid, though I see them less and less
I still maintain some hope for their resurgence nonetheless

So now I feel I've had my say of all that's on my mind
Regarding our humanity which God Himself designed
My dream is that we'll strive for what is honest, pure and true
And having shared these final thoughts, I bid you all adieu"

I turned and walked across the stage which now was turning dark
Convinced that my impassioned words had somehow missed their mark
But then I stopped and strained to hear a noise which gave me pause
It sounded like the echoes of a ghostly faint applause

Perhaps I'm not alone in these opinions I've expressed
Or in the faith and values that still burn within my breast
While some may think me foolish for this oratory role
There comes a time a man must rise and bare what's in his soul

Forsaken Heart

My heart is frail and cold tonight
Like orphans in the street
Who huddle in the alleyways
With rags about their feet

My heart is fraught and wounded
Like a deer within a snare
While peering from the darkness
Crouch the jackals of despair

My heart feels destitute tonight
Like sad and lonely men
Who dream of former glories
That will never come again

My heart no longer listens
For the sound of love's approach
The tapping of the horses' hooves
That draw flirtation's coach

Intimate Stranger

She watches as he's sleeping
While reclining by his side
He seems to her a stranger
Hiding thoughts he won't confide

She wonders what he's dreaming
As his lips betray a smile
She feels he feigns contentment
Guarding secrets all the while

Her fragile heart is troubled
Fighting fears she can't allay
Yet holding out the forlorn hope
That love will find a way

She watches as he's sleeping
In the stillness of the night
She longs to draw him near to her
And hold his body tight

Where once he was transparent
Now he's distant and withdrawn
There was a time she knew him well
But now those days are gone

She listens to his breathing
And the ticking of the clock
The door that guards his private thoughts
Is one she can't unlock

He may as well be absent now,
A thousand miles away
The chasm in his heart is one
She tries to bridge each day

She watches as he's sleeping
And she knows she's still in love
But wonders if she'll ever be
The one he's dreaming of

Mortal Soul

(Dedicated with respect and admiration to Edgar Allen Poe)

What fear this amber night instills
With echoed howls from distant hills
The forest rhythm out of tune
Beneath a blood-red gibbous moon

What bleak misfortune suffered I
Astride my horse while passing by
A shriek induced my steed to bolt
Which threw me for a headlong jolt

Alone within the forest heart
My fortitude did soon depart
And chills that dance upon my spine
Bespeak a dark, macabre design

The vines which slow my faltering pace
And limbs that scrape my pallid face
Advance the frightful creeping dread
Which slithers through my tortured head

Bedeviled by the shadows strange
That dance in eerie shapes deranged
My ears detect demented wails
From nigh beyond our earthly veils

Tormented by these sights and sounds
And stumbling as my heartbeat pounds
I madly tread the wooded path
In fear of vague and nameless wrath

128

Throughout the night I make my flight
Persisting on 'til dawn's first light
At last my fainting heart spies home
With gasping breath and feeble groans

And yet, what madness greets my eye
A shrouded scene 'neath morning's sky
I witness friends, on my approach,
Behind a horse-drawn funeral coach

My family crest hangs on the side
And in the crowd, my widowed bride
'Tis then I learned the awful toll,
Those woods had claimed my mortal soul

Reflections on Aging

As days and weeks accumulate becoming months and years,
I've learned to reconcile myself with life's concerns and fears
There's little point in fretting over things we can't control
Which only drains the spirit and debilitates the soul

I harbor no more grudges nor hold enmity towards men
I'd rather grant forgiveness than to walk those paths again
The days we have remaining are too few to soil with hate
Or waste in idle arguments and meaningless debate

I know the path that lies ahead is shorter than behind
This thought, though seldom spoken, is quite often on my mind
Yet still, I've made my peace with God and do not fear the end
He's granted me assurances this world can't comprehend

I often think of Heaven and the life that waits above
Since far too many tombstones bear the names of those I love
Some days I feel reflective, and at times I softly cry
For teardrops flow much easier than in those years gone by

I walk a little slower and my eyesight's not as keen
The product of an ample life and all the years between
But looking back, I'm grateful for those days of joy and bliss
Their memories sustain me as I walk and reminisce

Inside, I feel as youthful as I did in years before
Although the mirror confronts me with those truths I can't ignore
The price we pay for wisdom is inscribed upon our face
Those chronicled engravings in a script we can't erase

I wish our lives were longer for, at times, they seem so brief
The days pass by so quickly as I stare in disbelief
This quality of transience gives life its precious worth
A value it possesses from the moment of our birth

I've had my share of heartaches but I know that's nothing new
Each person has a story of the trials they've come through
Yet in the end, they only serve to make us who we are
We grow through tribulations though our souls may bear a scar

I harbor some regrets in life for errors and mistakes
My past contains embarrassments for which my heart still aches
I've pardoned all those trespasses from those whom once I knew
But granting self-forgiveness is more difficult to do

~

As days and weeks accumulate unveiling new frontiers,
I gaze outside my window and reflect on passing years
I haven't any pressing thoughts or counsel to impart
Except to not forsake the secret garden in your heart

Pieces of You
(*For Jill*)

Returning from the graveside, with my mother laid to rest
I could not help reflecting on her last heartfelt request
She had her nephew write this down before the final hour
A plea for family unity which long since had turned sour

"Be kind to one another, seek humility and peace
Let love restore relationships and grant you sweet release
Let go of old resentments and begin to forge new ties
Abandon pointless judgments and the need to criticize"

"My blood still courses through your veins uniting each with all
But pettiness and piety have built a daunting wall
And since my time upon this earth has come and gone at last
I ask you all to cast aside your conflicts from the past"

I wept from grief and heartache, yet still nodded in accord
I understood her sentiments (which largely were ignored)
Her final supplications fell on deaf and wooden ears
The sad results of stubbornness and folly through the years

The woeful days that followed served to further aggravate
As siblings and their offspring rummaged through my mom's estate
My eldest sister found me and endowed me with my share
A bracelet and some earrings with a necklace mom would wear

I held my tongue in silence with the process underway
And only delved infrequently into the painful fray
So when the week was over not a smidge had been ignored
While one by one my family members left with their reward

Though tears were shed and hugs were shared their comfort quickly
fades
As quickly I grew tired of their meaningless charades
No flood of empty platitudes can properly disguise
The shallowness of motives and indifference in their eyes

132

I spent the next week grieving with an emptiness inside
For mom had been a friend in whom I always could confide
The necklace set and bracelet are a heritage so dear
Yet greater still are memories that never disappear

Like weekends spent together or the phone calls late at night
The trips to see her grandkids which would fill us with delight
The times I sought her counsel and the times she set me straight
For years had brought her wisdom that mere youth can't duplicate

The time to show you love someone is when they're still alive
For no one knows the day and time their angel will arrive
So now I spend my evenings, when the moon is clear and bright,
Recalling conversations lasting deep into the night

Though other family members may have claimed a larger haul
I still retain possession of the greatest gift of all
Of all the things mom left behind in this reality
Surpassing jewels and artifacts, she shared *herself* with me

Days like this

On days like this I wonder how the earth still spins in space
While strewn across the landscape lie the dreams I used to chase
I wonder how the sun comes up and travels 'cross the sky
Like distant aspirations that proceed to pass me by

On nights like this I wonder how a wounded heart survives
Relentless storms of tempest winds that devastate our lives
Those prayers that go unanswered and the silence from above
All test our faith in providence and grace bestowed thereof

At times like this it's hard to rise and face another day
When azure skies seem blotted out by clouds of endless gray
The rain which falls through bleary haze reflects those tears inside
Which lie beneath the surface where a secret heart resides

On days like this I stare outside and sadly reminisce
Reflecting back on golden days of pure and simple bliss
I stir the dying embers of a love that once burned strong
And scan the vast horizon for a place where I belong

Night Rolls In

night rolls in
like a train station's
last arrival

passengers disembark
dispersing among
vacant heavens

the engine shudders
exhales
and is silent

the conductor refuels,
as a solitary headlight
shines forth

and illuminates the tracks
of tomorrow

You Tell Me That You Miss Me

You tell me that you miss me
And, in part, I'm sure that's true
The way an artist's brush might miss
A certain shade of blue

You miss me like a book you've read
That now just gathers dust
A tome from your collection
That's infrequently discussed

You miss me like a summer storm
That comes and goes so fast
So thrilling when the lightning strikes
Forgotten once it's passed

You miss me like a single star
That's absent from the sky
Whose vacancy is soon eclipsed
By brighter stars nearby

You miss me in the evening
When the shadows grow so long
When sadness overtakes you
And your loneliness is strong

But now, the world has called to me
And yearns to be explored
The station master cups his hands
And cries out "All Aboard"

136

The Sadness Overwhelming

My soul reflects the dreariness that permeates the day
The dull and languid emptiness that washes dreams away
The sad demise of hopefulness which downpours eulogize
And no lament or graveside grief can duly galvanize

My soul feels void of faith and trust, engulfed by endless pain
Adrift in Charon's paper boat down gutter streams of rain
It travels inexorably towards Hades' sewer grate
Where waterfalls convey it towards a subterranean fate

My soul is overwhelmed by all the sadness in this life
The loss of youthful innocence; hostility and strife
It echoes through my spirit like a church bell's distant knell
Or rusty flows of water from a cemetery well

The Road Home

Each day I tread this woodland road uncertain what I'll find
Enjoying nature's subtle charms and leaving cares behind
This evening as the shadows grow, they cast a pensive spell
And turn my thoughts to distant shores I used to know so well

So sweetly sings the nightingale to guide me on my way
And gently fades the crimson sun to usher out the day
While flowing brushstrokes paint a sky adorned with blue and gold
My mind reflects on times gone by as memories unfold

I think about my childhood days, so simple and sincere
Those echoes of Elysian joy still ripple through the years
The summers spent 'neath nurturing skies and starry nights so sweet
When all the world was in my grasp, my life felt so complete

I think of adolescent days and conflicts that they yield
With waves of passion breaching dams and flooding moral fields
Those sleepless nights of stubborn thoughts assessing one's self worth
Endeavoring to ascertain my place upon this earth

I contemplate those wayward steps beyond my years of youth
Pursuing vain elusive dreams, disdaining quests for truth
I think of words my parents spoke and lessons they'd impart
But seldom did those seeds take root within my shallow heart

As daylight flees from twilight skies and ebon night birds soar
I travel down this well-worn path much further than before
A soothing breeze enfolds the dusk with arms of quiet grace
And bids me stay in musing thought amidst its cool embrace

My mind reflects on those I hurt and others I ignored
Relationships I cast aside to never be restored
I think of opportunities and chances that I spurned
Of bridges that I should have crossed and others that I burned

Throughout my summer years of life I cared not what was lost
And even though the price was high I'd rarely count the cost
Then came a day of recompense, I found myself alone
And learned, too late, no gardens grow where bitter winds have blown

I wish I could go back and change the damage that's been done
But time flows ever forward and amends its course for none
So now I spend my autumn days upon this wooded trail
In silent contemplation of the life beyond this veil

I follow as the road, at length, begins to turn and wind
Attracted by a call that whispers faintly in my mind
Afar, I view a dwelling where the path appears to end
Which beckons to my soul in ways I barely comprehend

In drawing near, my heart begins to leap within my chest
My heavy burdens lifting as I reach my journey's crest
For at the gate, the hidden truth reveals itself at last
As in the lamp-lit windows stand the loved ones from my past

I see their faces clearly in the lanterns' amber glow
Their eyes reflecting mercy as my tears begin to flow
I've missed them all so dearly in the years since they've been gone
But now my shame and fear dispel within the breaking dawn

The Shepherd then unlocks the gate and bids me come inside
While one by one my family members join me by my side
Through all the years I've traveled and the pathways that I'd roam
I've found, at last, redemption in the joy of coming home

Appendix

Appendix (cont.)

Appendix (cont.)

www.ingramcontent.com/pod-product-compliance
Lightning Source LLC
Chambersburg PA
CBHW060208070426
42447CB00035B/2846